I F*cking Hate Zoom Quizzes

A collection of poems about Covid-19, the year 2020, and beyond

M.J. Edwards

For the readers
You're all lovely

Contents

Introduction
by Richard Edwards

What can I say about my mum? She's passionate, creative, and she loves her new venture as a writer. Yes, she may have written three *interesting* books, but you cannot deny the fact that she pours love and energy into those stories like no author I know (I know 2).

Since my father left her for Aunt Diane and they moved to the Isle of Wight (taking mum's ferrets with them — but that's a story for another time) she has spent time with me in my home, with my wife and children, continuing to put pen to paper (but mainly a keyboard) to entertain the people who have bought, rented — and most importantly read — her books.

Whilst I find the erotica she writes frustrating, one of her first ventures into the literary world was via writing poetry. Some of it is excellent. Some of it is different. But it's all worth a read. That's why I encouraged her to put together the poems she's written over the past year and a half, and share them with you all.

The collection you are about to read is raw with emotion. An outpouring of love, lust (mum, I'm not comfortable saying that tbh), hurt and hatred.

Mum loves what she does. She loves that people share her work in YouTube videos, TikTok's, Twitter posts and every other social platform where people have shared her stories. She loves the outpouring of feedback—both the good and the not so good—and she loves that people are enjoying what she does. Keep at it, mum. Keep making people smile.

mum don't put this bit in my intro but you def should edit out the poem about the pizza place because it's a bit too bloody weird even for you ok? I'll give you a ring later x

2020
a poem by M.J. Edwards

Fuck you, fuck you, fuck you
Fuck you, fuck you, fuck you
Fuck you, fuck you, fuck you
Fuck you, fuck you, fuck you.

Fuck you, fuck you, fuck you
Fuck you, fuck you, fuck you
Fuck you, fuck you, fuck you
Fuck you, fuck you, fuck you.

Fuck you, fuck you, fuck you
Fuck you, fuck you, fuck you
Fuck you, fuck you, fuck you
Fuck you, fuck you, fuck you.

Rage (Fire and War)
a poem by M.J. Edwards

Fresh breath drawn in to a brand new year,
Like the young lungs of a waking mouse,
You promised us so much,
You said 'this is mine'
Yet little did we know,
Other plans had been made.

The man in the chair,
His anger billowing like a rampant moon,
Wage war and hatred on a man he has not met.
He hast not met.
A nation of men he does not know.

Fire rains down from the sky.
Hatred reins from the man in the chair.
But why?
For what reason?
Nobody but him shall know.

But ho, t'was not the only fire.
In another land, one souther than south,
Another type of battle had begun.
One with nature.
And one with pain.

Flora, fauna, animal, man.
Locked together in a ferocious clash.
Crackle and bang as the flames grasped at life.
Then that life,
Was no longer life at all.

Humanity cursed this turbulent start.
To a year which promised us the earth.
One down, eleven to go.
The rest would be so much better,
What fools we were.

Note by author M.J. Edwards: just to be clear, this is about the Australian wildfires and the US bombing Iraq in January 2020

Lockdown
a poem by M.J. Edwards

STAY HOME, they yell,
Do not leave your houses.
Don't touch, wash well,
Be as quiet as two mouses.

Everyone is cut off,
From a world once wide and there,
All it takes is a cough,
To cause a sudden scare.

Not me, they say,
They defy the order,
Come what may,
They're now a toilet roll hoarder.

They bake banana bread,
They workout to Joe Wicks,
Whilst thousands lay down dead,
They have no flour for their cake mix.

People lose their jobs,
People are furloughed,
We become a world of slobs,
We think that we are owed.

No football on the telly,
A spouse fed up with me.
His ever growing belly,
More banana bread for tea.

For months we wait without
our loved ones and our friends,
A spring of a love drought,
Hoping that it ends.

Lost
a poem by M.J. Edwards

I am a good employee,
I work hard and fast and great,
I never moan or take sick days,
I hardly ever show up late.

One time I accidentally stole,
A box of leather binders,
But I brought half back to you,
After just fourteen reminders.

I always meet my KPI's,
Apart from May and June,
And July and March and April,
But I know I'll improve soon.

You didn't mind when you found out,
I'd been gambling during lunch,
Or when Debbie Smith and I fought,
Though she did deserve that punch.

I'm sorry about the time I slept,
During the big client on-board meeting,
I'm sorry I wanked in the toilet,
A phase that was just fleeting.

You see I was rather sex starved,
You just weren't meant to see.
And I didn't intend on my vibrator
falling in your tea.

You called me to your office, and
You told me to go home.
You blamed it on the virus,
But we know the reason, Jerome.

The yeast infection in your eye,
Just couldn't be my fault.
Just because you drank the tea,
You said it's me just by default.

So here I am, the world in tatters,
I have no job, no hope at all,
I apply and beg and wait all day,
But no one will return my call.

Clap for Carers
Flash fiction by M.J. Edwards

George stands beside his wife, Jennifer, in the doorway of their home. It's a nice home. It has a grey door, much like their hair, yet the wood is smooth, unlike their wrinkled skin. They both nod to Mr McMuck at number twenty-eight across the road, who has also chosen to stand in his own doorway, in what has now become a weekly routine. A few doors down, in either direction (although George doesn't know their name… one of them is Dan maybe?), other neighbours do the same. A lady is dressed in her pyjamas and another man is wearing no shirt at all. Shocking.

They all bang their hands together like seals who are begging for scraps of fish at a fish market. They've been told it's the right thing to do. The best thing to do. The only thing they can do.

They've been led to believe that if they do that (same time, same place, like an unwanted puppet show), the terrible virus will go away and more lives will be saved — and yet here it remains.

It's nought but a gesture. A crashing of waves carried by the wind that, once the wind dies down, so does the gesture.

It's appreciation, they say. It shows that they understand the sacrifices the men and women who put themselves on the line, day after day, are doing for them. They expect them to believe that it isn't money or benefits or safety they crave — but a round of applause like a circus clown fresh from sculpting a balloon shaped-giraffe.

George clapped every week. Like a good boy.

Until Jennifer was no longer there to clap alongside him.

Then he clapped no more.

He clapped no more.

Then the next week she did clap with him again because they moved Eastenders back an hour.

You're on Mute
a poem by M.J. Edwards

What is there to do,
When the world decides to close?
I'll sit and watch TV,
Or masturbate, I suppose.

Or, here's a fun idea,
We'll get together on Zoom,
Back then, it sounded great,
But now… fills me with doom.

Bad connection, dropping off,
Auntie Lilly starts to jerk,
Not in a rude way of course,
Her internet won't work.

Uncle Jeff has done a quiz,
But can't work out unmute,
Everyone talks over me,
Oh look a cat! How cute.

So yes, Zoom quizzes were,
A great way to spend a night,
But now, more than a year on,
All they do is fill me with fright.

I never want to see,
Another Zoom quiz that's for sure,
So please, dear scientists, please,
Hurry up and find a bloody cure.

Six Months
a poem by M.J. Edwards

SIX MONTHS.
That's how long it's been.
SIX MONTHS.
Since anyone has kissed me.

SIX MONTHS.
Since I have seen a penis.
SIX MONTHS.
It's not my lack of keenness.

SIX MONTHS.
I'm sitting, watching the clock.
SIX MONTHS.
Since I tickled a cock.

SIX MONTHS.
Since he last looked at me.
SIX MONTHS.
And every day I plea.

SIX MONTHS.
Since you started going out.
SIX MONTHS.
You've been having doubt.

TODAY.
You told me we were done.
TODAY.
You've packed your bags and gone.

SIX MONTHS.
Since the day that you first kissed her.
SIX MONTHS.
You've been in love with my sister

Sitting On My Golden Balcony
a poem by M.J. Edwards

As the world slowly closes.
As people shut up shop,
As mankind panics,
As people suffer,
You are there for us.

You light up the silver screen,
You write and act and sing,
You have an army of followers,
You tell us about your life,
We see you day by day.

We see your hillside mansion,
We hear your tales of worry,
We watch you stand by with us,
We wonder if it's real.
A paradise amongst the weeds.

A place you call your home,
A sprawling, modern estate,
A car in every garage,
A pool you swim in daily,
As you say you are with us.

Key Workers
a poem by M.J. Edwards

Hello there, Mr Supermarket Man,
I see you, stocking shelves, as fast as you can,

Good morning, Mrs Doctor Nurse,
You're here, helping, during this terrible curse.

What ho, Mr Delivery Driver,
You're working hard, here's a tip (a fiver).

Hiya love, Ms Warehouse Staff,
Working twelve hour shifts, are you having a laugh?

Guten Tag, Dear Chef,
Cooking, cleaning, complains only to the deaf.

Our weatherman, our postman, the bus driver, the
plumber,
You don't know furlough, you worked all through
summer.

Thank you for being here, for doing your best.
Thank you for working, looking after the rest.

Whoops
a poem by M.J. Edwards

Our fearless leaders, the men to whom we look to,
They make the hard choices, they call the shots,
Question science, listen to God, tell you what to do.

I will shake the hand of man and woman, they say,
They visit the wards, they keep their word,
Then what should happen soon after? Dismay.

The leader on the island, his hair a shock of white,
He falls so gravely ill, he is taken at once to bed,
They tell us in the news, he may not make it through
the night.

It is a long and turbulent road, but pulls through he
does,
Then back to smiling, waving, putting on the show,
Anything to create that winning media buzz.

Then across the sea, the man who divides,
Copies the shock of white, does not learn,
And tests come back true, then he runs and hides.

History repeats, the men who call the shots,
Not well, not well at all, very unwell in fact.
Yet for some reason, they cannot connect the dots.

Listen to the men with stethoscopes on their necks,
They know the charts, they know the math,
They are not playing with lives for more zeros on their
cheques.

Oh, Chris Whitty
a poem by M.J. Edwards

Oh Chris Whitty,
You really are so pretty.
With your cute white shirts,
You bum, so pert,
The media treats you shitty.

You stand up on that podium,
As the world around us emplodium.
They call you gloom,
They say you're doom.
In our wounds you rub some sodium.

But it isn't your fault, Chris,
You aren't taking the piss.
You give us facts,
Tell us the tacts,
As everything goes amiss.

I love your cute, red tie,
It helps me to get by,
It feels like such a tease
When you say 'next slide please',
You make me feel so shy.

Your job is hard, we know that,
You cannot win, with your chat.
Keep on trucking,
You'll get some luck in,
All cos some guy ate a bat.

Streaming
a poem by M.J. Edwards

Twenty four hours in a day,
Eight is owned by sleep.
Two is owned by eating.
One is owned by grooming.
Half an hour is owned by masturbation
(maybe an hour, depends on the day)
And that leaves the remaining twelve.

What do we do?

What
do
we
do?

The television, of course.
We can always count on telly.

We sit on our backsides,
We have our founds perpetually

GLUED

to our hands like our lives only have meaning
if we are playing Angry Birds or on TikTok

or PORNOGRAPHY

Trapped within four walls, we can always

count
on
telly.

Tiger King was there, we laughed we were shook
we didn't believe he was real. Why would he not be
real?

He is the king of tigers.

A Queen who plays chess.
Who knew chess could be so interesting?

Not I, I says. Not I.

Nor men in suits who refuse to show their faces.
Such a beautiful face. And space battles.
Or Marvel characters called Wanda and Vision,
you put the name together and you get the name
WANDAVISION
It's like television but with the character, because
that's sort of how the show works (spoiler).

But we binge. We winge. I get a tinge,
of jealousy when I'm done, because others will
now get to see it for the first time and I cannot.

But wait. Kobra Kai. It's like the Karate Kid,
except old, and it shouldn't be good,

YES IT IS.

So we binge and we winge and then once again.

The tinge.

But do not fear,
There will be something new again. Something near.
Don't shed a tear.

Black Lives Matter
a poem by M.J. Edwards

When I first heard black lives matter, I was confused,
I thought, "don't all lives matter?"

But then I realised, I once gave money to *Save the Rainforest,*
But I didn't think "don't all forests matter?"

Then I didn't think the first thing anymore.

**Goodbye
Haikus by M.J. Edwards**

You said you loved me,
But it was all a damn lie,
You just love yourself.

How could you do it?
Lay there with her in my bed,
Whilst I cried downstairs.

I'm sure it wasn't me.
The infection was from you.
I am sure of it.

I know it's true now.
I got tested and confirmed.
Your yeast. Your disease.

And her. That shit bitch.
My own fucking sister, man.
So off you can fuck.

Oh god, why god why,
The pain you have caused me, nob,
I am free from you.

Eat Out to Help Out
a poem by M.J. Edwards

This was all just one big misunderstanding, a slip up, a
goof, a mistake,
A government scheme intended to get us eating chips
and pizza and cake.

Eat Out To Help Out, they said, a catchy phrase, and
one quite clear enough,
Except for me, because it turns out, it doesn't mean to
lick a muff.

Yes, I admit, this past few months I've been
experimenting, letting loose, but,
I got to talking to a nice lady I met during a nice lunch
at a Pizza Hut,

And one thing led to another, we got to talking, and
then who could have guessed,
After one or three too many wines, her hand slid down
and grabbed my breast.

We kissed right there by the salad bar, I felt a rush like
no other, a incredible twinge,
We headed to a booth by the window, and then,
somehow, I ate her minge.

I'd never seen another vagina before, they don't exactly
look the prettiest,
But she moaned and groaned and writhed so I can't
have been the shittiest.

The manager came and asked us to leave, but I made
sure I finished first,
We fled on foot, but the police found us, I guess I must
be cursed.

Thankfully there was no evidence, no other diners, the
CCTV was bust,
So after answering some questions, they let us go,
which did wonders for my lust.

But gone, was the woman from the Pizza Hut, taking
her vagina with her,
Thanks for my brief, wonderful encounter, I think I
may just miss her.

Tears for Tiers
a poem by M.J. Edwards

The fear is real
The fear of the tier.

Whether two or three,
Or the whore that is four.

First the south, then the north,
Sharing the crown of tiered lockdown.

Christmas is cancelled,
Giving gifts causing rifts.

Then BAM the tiers go,
We're all fools under new national rules.

But for how long?
Nobody knows. The country is closed.

Single Girl
a poem by M.J. Edwards
(Read to the tune of Barbie Girl, by Aqua)

I'm a single girl, in a covid world,
Life indoors, it's so poor.
You can't hug me tight, just stay home and read
Twilight
What a shit show, life right now sure does blow.

I'm a mid-fifties girl, in a post-covid world
Lock me down, make it tight, it's so shitty
No more fun, no more sun, just the same drab four
walls,
Takeaways, more TV, wanky wanky.

You can't touch,
You can't play,
You can say, I'm always bored (Ooh oh)

I'm a single girl, in a covid world,
Life indoors, it's so poor.
You can't hug me tight, just stay home and read
Twilight
What a shit show, life right now sure does blow.

This pandemic, so systemic
(screw this lockdown)
This pandemic, so systemic
(Ooh ooh oh, ooh ooh oh)

This pandemic, so systemic
(screw this lockdown)

This pandemic, so systemic
(Ooh ooh oh, ooh ooh oh)

I'm a single girl, in a covid world,
Life indoors, it's so poor.
You can't hug me tight, just stay home and read
Twilight
What a shit show, life right now sure does blow.

etc.

Tears for Tears 2
a poem by M.J. Edwards

ONE
Rule of six.
Do not mix.
Go to work.
Don't be a berk.

TWO
Kind of the same,
In fact exactly the same.
Why does it exist?
Shouldn't be on the list.

THREE
Meet only outdoors,
And for a good cause.
Close all the pubs,
Except for takeaway grubs.

FOUR
Everything's shut,
Hair remains uncut,
Christmas no more,
The dreaded tier four.

**Dear Mr President
a poem by M.J. Edwards**

Dear Mr President,
Hello, my name is Ms Edwards,
and I live in a small country called the UK.
It's on the other side of the ocean,
Somewhere close to Italy and Latvia,
We eat cheese on toast for supper,
and sometimes drink coffee but mainly 7UP.
I heard you and another man are fighting,
you call each other names and
you're both old, but want the same job.
One of you is possibly racist,
the other one inappropriate around women,
but one of you is worse than the other one,
and I'm not sure which.
I'm not sure which.
You live in a big house,
which looks very nice on the television,
but I've never visited it myself,
although I did see it explode
on Independence Day.
Have you ever met Bill Pullman?
He was a nice President.
I would totally vote for him if I were American,
but that film was sad because he had a dead wife,
and your wife looks like she hates you.
Have you seen Independence Day?
If you haven't, I think you should watch it.
Bill Pullman did a good speech in it.
And Will Smith has nice ears.
And the man from Star Trek is funny in it.

And there's a dog in it, called Boomer.
Boomer has become a bit of a naughty word,
hasn't it, Mr President?
Could you do something to stop it?
One of my sisters is called Karen, and she is also a
boomer,
so she doesn't like it.
But she's a bitch so that's fine.
Please send me your address and I'll,
post you a DVD of Independence Day.
It's a box set with the second one,
but that isn't very good so you don't have to watch that
one.
Thank you, Mr President, for reading my letter.
You must be very busy, but maybe your aide,
will read you my letter as you golf.
Or when you pause Independence Day,
to Tweet something.

Auntie Vax (is Coming to Town)
a Poem by M.J. Edwards

"You better not jab,
Or else you will cry,
What they made in that lab,
Will make your brain fry."
Auntie Vax is coming to town.

She's making up the news,
she shared on Facebook:
That her mate Jean had hers and it made her face stuck,
Auntie Vax is coming to town.

She loves whinging, complaining,
She hates scientific fact,
Despite having botox last year,
Which made her forehead cracked,

OH!

"You better no take,
that vaccine," she warned,
"It'll make your bones ache,
And you will not be mourned."
Auntie Vax is coming to town.

**The Big Blue Bus
a poem by M.J. Edwards**

*Note from the author, M.J. Edwards: Since writing this poem
I have discovered that the bus wasn't blue, it was actually
red, so please disregard any references to it being red. I didn't
want to change it though, because Big Blue Bus is a much
nicer title.*

Such a magical sight,
Rolling the streets, granting wishes,
Like the devil, promising riches at the cost of a soul,
The big blue bus.

The big blue bus tricked me,
Oh how it pulled the wool over my eyes.
It lied, it lied, it lied.
It is a bus, which told so many lies.

Money for the NHS, they said
Two-hundred million extra a week,
But the big blue bus had a secret,
It was a liar, disguised as a bus.

And we fell for it. The majority.
The big blue bus of magic,
The clock cannot be turned back,
And now I cannot get any lettuce.

Chairs cost more to buy,
I cannot sell things on eBay to Ireland,
The world basically hates us.
And for what, big blue bus, for what?

**New Year, New Me
a poem by M.J. Edwards**

I'm done with this bullshit,
I'm at the end of my whit,
When midnight comes,
A new me becomes,
And time to stop acting like a tit.

I want to become someone strong.
I need to find a place to belong.
No more messing,
And no more stressing,
The clock strikes twelve; **dong**.

I wake up on January first,
With so much energy I could burst,
I run downstairs,
Shower and comb my hairs,
I could take on the world with a thirst.

What should I do, where to go?
I want to lead, not to follow,
I put on my shoes,
Whilst watching the news,
Then out the door fast, not slow.

I march and walk miles and miles,
My chest puffed out, face full smiles,
I can take on the Earth,
Or for what it is worth,
At least the south of the British Isles.

But then, oh my God, I do say,
As the sky is all cloudy and grey,
I stop dead my strut
The shops are all shut,
Everything's closed 'cos it's New Years Day.

So I go back to the house like a clown,
As my smile turns into a frown.
I guess I can't change,
Which is ever so strange,
So I put on the TV and sit down.

The Storm
a poem by M.J. Edwards

Winds rush,
But not the winds of winter,
The winds of hate.

Thunder strikes,
But not the thunder of storm clouds,
The thunder of anger.

Waves crash,
But not deep ocean waves,
Waves of mob mentality.

People scream,
But not fun happy time screams,
Screams of terror.

People hide,
But not because they're playing hide and seek,
They're hiding for their lives.

People sit in chairs,
But not their own chairs,
The chairs of congress-people.

People gloat,
But not because they won at Monopoly,
Because they think they've won at life.

But they haven't won.
They're silly.

Dear Mr New President
Flash fiction by M.J. Edwards

Dear Mr President,

I hope you don't mind me writing. I wrote to your predecessor, but he never wrote back, so I'm hoping I have a little more success with you. You claim you'll work much harder than the last president, rather than play lots of golf on the golf course, so I'm confident I should hear back from you within ten working days. Email is fine, or a text if you're pushed for time.

I've seen you on the TV. You sometimes lose your patients (*patience, mum, he's not a doctor*) and you like to sniff ladies hairs, which is a little weird, but you still seem a lot better than the last one who was very angry all the time, like a snapping crocodile at Gatorland in Florida, which I visited in 2002 with my husband and son before one left me and the other moved out. I'll let you figure out which is which, but the outcome is still the same.

Anyway, this isn't about me. It's about you. I just want to wish you luck. Being the president seems like a very tough job, and I should know, I was put in charge of arranging my friend Amanda's baby shower and it was a right shit show in the end, so to arrange a whole country must be at least five times harder.

When you come to the UK, I'd like to take you to lunch. Please say yes. If going out isn't your thing, Morrisons do a lovely afternoon tea for two for £10 which is a bargain, but let me know ahead of time because sometimes you have to book it.

Good luck, Mr President. You have a kind face, like a man who sells Ice Cream at Disney World (which I also visited in 2002), so I have every faith you will be a good president. I also think you'll make a good animatronic president in the Hall of Presidents, which is an attraction at Disney World.

Have you been to Disney World?

Thank you for taking the time to read my letter, Mr President. I might not be able to impart you with wisdom, like similar letters you have received from other world leaders, but I at least hope you found it a little bit goofy (a character I met at Disney World!)

Yours kindly,
M.J. Edwards

**Vaccine Roll Out
a poem by M.J. Edwards**

They said it couldn't be done.
And yet, here you all are.
Every day, you jab our arms.
People come from near and far.

The vaccine drive is underway,
They roll out like Optimus Prime,
The NHS are doing their thing,
You simply are sublime.

Never mind Optimus Prime,
You're making me *Optimistic Prime*,
Sticking the vaccine in us,
In what has been a difficult climb.

I had my arm done on Tuesday,
I felt a little iffy and went to bed,
But by Thursday I was right as rain,
And felt good, because I wouldn't be dead.

So from me, to you, please listen,
The doctors know what they're saying,
Go and get that jab in your arm,
And slash the number the virus is slaying.

The Ferrets
a poem by M.J. Edwards

You took my babies from me
You bastard.

You don't even like them
You bastard.

You just did it to hurt me
You bastard.

Their furry little noses,
Their beady little eyes,
Like snakes, but fluffy, and with legs.

I loved them all, like I birthed them myself,
And you snatched them away
In the dead of night,
Like the Hamburgler prowling McDonalds' kitchen.

You bastard.

And then, I'm shocked to discover,
You released them into the wild,
And now, the Isle of Wight,
Has a population of ferrets, they did not ask for.

They didn't ask for them at all.
You bastard.

But alas, come hither, pip pip,
I will have the last laugh.

Because I went to the pet shop,
Oh yes I did.

And I have a new baby of my own.
Huzzah.
I say,
I have a new baby of my own.
He is called Chump.

You bastard.

About the Author

M.J. Edwards is in the process of rebuilding her life, thanks to the kind support of the people who continue to read her books.

She is currently living in a studio flat with Chump (although the landlord doesn't know about him) and likes to set up fake Facebook accounts to send unflattering messages to her sister and soon-to-be-ex-husband.

She loves Chump very much.

Follow her on Twitter @MJEdwardsAuthor